THE PEER PARTNERS HANDBOOK

THE PEER PARTNERS HANDBOOK

Helping Your Friends Live Free from Violence, Drug Use, Teen Pregnancy & Suicide

Jerry Kreitzer & David Levine

A guide for students in leadership programs

Station Hill

Published by Station Hill Press, Inc.
Barrytown, New York 12507

Cover design by Susan Quasha
Illustrations by Nick Jones

Design implementation by K • V • S GRAPHICS

Library of Congress Cataloging-in-Publication Data

Kreitzer, Jerry.
  The peer partners handbook : helping your friends live free from violence, drug use, teen pregnancy & suicide : a guide to students in leadership programs / Jerry Kreitzer & David Levine.
      p.   cm.
  ISBN 0-88268-195-8
  1. Teenagers--Counseling of--Study and teaching--United States.
  2. Peer counseling--Study and teaching--United States.   I. Levine, David, 1959- . II. Title.
  HV1431.K74 1995
  362.7'083--dc20   95-24134
                                                              CIP

Dedication

To all the peer leaders with whom we have been fortunate to work and whose desire to help others is a constant source of inspiration and hope to us.

Special Thanks

To the people who have been our teachers, guides and mentors:
Tom Turney, Marsha Brown, Bob Barrette, Ricia McMahon and Jerry Edwards. Your caring and devotion to the lives of young people really does make a difference. We have enjoyed our times together.

To Ann Godesky, advisor to the Pawling Peer Program, Pawling High School, Pawling, New York and Joan Ayotte, advisor to the Student Bridges Peer Program, Shea High School, Pawtucket, Rhode Island for the wonderful quotations and reflections from your students.

To the students in the Peer to Peer Program at Rutland High School, Rutland, Vermont for your insights about peer leadership.

Also to Devi Paolillo Levine for your patience, insight, friendship and love.

JK & DL

SOME THOUGHTS ON STUDENT LEADERSHIP PROGRAMS

"Living as a youth in today's society you are confronted with overwhelming issues and decisions.

That's why being a peer leader is so essential. As a peer leader you are a mentor, someone who tries their best to show others how to make difficult decisions. A peer leader is someone who is constantly encouraging and helping others succeed. It is giving others the same tools you have acquired. Being a peer leader is my way of contributing to make our world a better place."

Brenda Nimoh

Age 16, is a member of Shea High School's "Student Bridges Peer Program", Pawtucket, Rhode Island.

From the country of Ghana.

"I'm glad that a lot of people are starting to see how important peer leadership is. If anyone has the opportunity to do something like this, they should go for it."

Bryan Goodchild

Age 17, is a member of Rutland High School's "Peer To Peer" program, Rutland, Vermont.

"Students are really the only ones who understand each other. They should stick together and help each other out."

Melissa Basler

Age 17, is a member of Pawling High School's "Peer Leadership Program", Pawling, New York.

"I think that if only one program were put into my country or any other country, this should be it. It would help many students who quit from the school to become members of gangs, robbers, drug addicts, and many other things. They don't care about school.

After this they became a problem at their house because they didn't respect their parents and sometimes they fought with their parents. I say all this because I was one of them. I quit school, I was a gang member. All this is stupid, but I did these things only to try to get friends and feel good.

Now I know the good way and thank other students and a lot of people who help in this country. I feel very good about what I do now in peer leadership with other students. I want to be someone in this life and help students who need help, students who don't have any orientation, and students who use drugs.

When people ask me why I am concerned about other people and not of myself, I say I'm concerned about others because we are all humans, we are all brothers and sisters. We have to help one another. "

Marlon Garcia

Age 17, is a member of Shea High School's "Student Bridges" peer program, Pawtucket, Rhode Island.

From the country of Guatemala.

"Not only have I learned how important it is to work with other students peacefully but I also leave every meeting/event with a sense of accomplishment."

Mokanna Cooper

Age 16, is a member of Shea High School's "Student Bridges" peer program, Pawtucket, Rhode Island.

"By working with other people I've been able to bring out a more open side of myself."

Wade Mclaughlin

Age 17, is a member of Rutland High School's "Peer To Peer" program, Rutland, Vermont.

✎ CONTENTS ✎

WELCOME FROM THE AUTHORS

If you are currently involved in running activities with your peers as part of a student leadership program, we have written this guide for you.

This is not a text book with complex theories and in-depth philosophies. Instead, it's a guide to be used as a resource when working with groups of other young people. You will find specifics on the **how to's** for the following:

- **Preparing to make a presentation to your peers**
- **Organizing your thoughts into a presentation**
- **Communicating effectively with others**
- **Developing your own principles of leadership**

No matter what your school's program is called: peer leadership, peer mediation, peer education, peer helping, peer mentoring or student council, it is important to develop communication and facilitation skills if you want to work with others and help them. Skills for working with others seem basic, but often are hard to find when you need them most. This book offers activities to help you become more effective when working with others. As we observe how powerful young people can be when they provide positive modeling while working with their peers, it makes us wonder what this world could be if every community, school and youth group would offer opportunities for students to take leadership roles. We hope that *The Peer Partners Handbook* will be helpful to you on your journey. The future is yours.

Enjoy!
Jerry Kreitzer & David Levine

WHO THE PEER PARTNERS HANDBOOK IS FOR

This guide is for any student (Grades 9–12) who is or will be working with other students in the following situations:

- Peer mediation
- Church groups
- Youth Groups
- Big brother/big sister
- Theatre groups
- AIDS education
- Peer tutoring programs
- Student council
- Camp couselors
- Scouting
- Teen institute
- Peer mentoring
- Resident Assistants in college dormitories
- Peer leadership workshops/classes
- International student gatherings
- SADD (Students Against Drunk Driving)
- School clubs/organizations
- Alcohol and other drug prevention programs
- Junior fraternal organizations
- Safety programs: bicycle, fire prevention, school bus

NICK JONES

I

Working With Your Peers

"Peer Leadership helped me accomplish many victories which eventually will help me accomplish my goals in the real life, the future."

Claudio Santos, age 17, is a member of Shea High School's "Student Bridges" peer leadership program in Pawtucket, Rhode Island.

I. WORKING WITH YOUR PEERS

Today, many students are doing wonderful things with their peers and you are probably one of them. More and more, school personnel are beginning to realize that the most under-utilized resources for helping young people in schools are the students themselves.

The Peer Partners Handbook is for young people like your-self who want to take a leadership role in helping make the world a better place for their peers.

Throughout this book we use the term "peer leadership" to refer to student leadership programs. We also will use the name "peer leaders" for those who are members of a peer leadership program.

We define peers as:

> **Those in your same age group as well as younger students with whom you might be working.**

We define leadership as:

> * **Maximizing the involvement of those you want to influence**.

This guide offers you our vision of how to work successfully with your peers. It contains specific knowledge to help you as you work with others. It will help you understand how groups function, and give you some tools to use when leading a group through a learning experience.

We've written *The Peer Partners Handbook* with the strong belief that with guidance and support people who care, like yourself, can make a difference that goes beyond words and on into positive actions.

> * *Definition of leadership is from* Peer Leadership, *written and published by Thomas Turney.*

"The program has really made me more out-going and more trusting of my peers."

Natasha Schwartz, age 16, Pawling High School, Pawling, N.Y.

We believe that with the necessary skills, support and trust, you can make a significant difference in the lives of the other young people around you.

We hope that as you experience the many joys and rewards of working with others, the skills you develop will carry beyond your years in school and be with you wherever and whenever you are interacting with people, which is forever.

"Peer leadership has enabled me to explore my own talents, build up my self-esteem, as well as create values and goals for myself."

Jayne Harrington, age 17, Pawling High School, Pawling, N.Y.

A. PREPARING FOR THE PRESENTATION

Peer leaders are called upon to do many things in and out of school, one of which is to make presentations to groups of people. Many find this one of their greatest challenges.

When you make a presentation as a peer leader, you might find yourself anxious or scared. This is natural and expected, so if you've ever felt this way you're not alone. Let's go through the experience of making a presentation to a group of students.

CONGRATULATIONS!

Today you are presenting to a group of students. As you wake up and get out of bed you discover something: your palms are sweaty, your heart is beating rapidly, you don't feel well. I guess you could say you're nervous.

A million questions run through your mind:

> *What if they don't listen to me? What if they don't like me? What if I forget what I'm going to say? What if they get rowdy? How will I remember their names? Will I do a good job? Will I actually help them? What should I wear? Why am I doing this at all?*

Whenever you have so many questions and concerns swimming in your head, ask yourself two questions:

What am I thinking?
What am I feeling?

Let's try it...

What am I thinking?

"What is going to happen today with my peers?"
"Will I do a good job?"
"Will I actually help them?"
"Will they like me?"

What am I Feeling?

"My palms are sweaty."
"I'm nervous and scared."

The two questions *"what am I thinking"* and *"what am I feeling"* will help "focus" you whenever you feel a little out of sync. It is important to get yourself together first, so that you can focus on the group's needs and not your own.

Once you are centered and "in control" of your feelings, you are ready for the next step: the presentation itself. The following pages will help you plan and implement a presentation to a group of your peers.

16

B. ORGANIZING YOUR THOUGHTS INTO A LESSON

Okay, so you're setting up for a lesson (a presentation to a group of your peers).

There are four things to consider:

1) Identifying your goal: What do you want to accomplish?

2) Framing the experience: How will you begin the experience?

3) Reaching your goal: How will you accomplish your goal with the group?

4) Coming to closure: How will you end the experience?

Carrying out these four components will help you to provide a complete experience for the students, no matter what lesson you are teaching or who you are working with.

Let's explore these in detail:

First...

1) Identify your goal: what do you want to accomplish?

The most effective presentations are those which do not attempt to do too much.

Pick one main point and teach it well.

If you can teach one main point to the group, you have reached your goal.

As you identify your goal, it is vital to understand the topic you are covering. Sometimes the topic is selected for you. The guidance department, for instance, may ask a group of students to work with freshmen who are new to the school. In this case, the topic or program is "handed" to you. It is called: **Freshman Orientation.**

You must also determine who you are working with (the population) and how many there will be. In our example, you might be working with twenty in-coming freshmen.

Here's another example: Two of you are asked to do a presentation for twenty-five fifth grade students on bicycle safety.

- The *topic* is **bicycle safety**

- The *population* is **fifth grade students**

- The *number* of students is **twenty-five**

The goal of your session might be that "every student will understand how important it is to wear a helmet whenever they ride a bicycle, even if it's 'just down the street.'"

Once your goal is identified, you must ask yourself "How will I start the lesson?" It is important to **stay clear and focused.** The beginning provides the first impression for your peers. The next page introduces how to "Frame the experience."

2) Framing the Experience.

In the beginning of a presentation, you must frame the experience for the students.

Framing means to give a clear and specific introduction to the group at the beginning of a presentation or lesson. It's like giving a snapshot of what is about to be discussed, experienced or learned.

At the circus, the ringmaster is continually "framing" experiences for the audience.

"Ladies and gentlemen! If you look at the trapeze above, you will soon see the Flying Wallendas do triple somersaults into the mouth of a lion."

Or something like that.

The purpose of **framing** is to help everyone feel as relaxed as possible so that they can focus on the skills presented, rather than on their fear of the unknown.

From the beginning, you must give the group *specific, nonthreatening information.* This is what framing is all about. Successful framing can be the difference between success or failure with a group.

Here's an effective way to frame a potentially scary experience:

"Today we are going to work on the communication skill of listening."

"This might be hard for some of you but we will support you through the process."

"Our first task will be to find a partner."

In this example the students have been told exactly what the goal of the session is: *"To work on the* **communication skill** *of listening."* They also have been told that the peer leaders **will support them** through the process.

Here's another way to frame the same experience, one which might make it difficult for you to have success with the students.

> *"Okay, we're going to work on communication. Stand up and find a partner."*

Immediately, some students will feel "put on the spot."

> *"Uh oh, now I have to find a partner. I don't like this."*

In this example students are potentially "set up" to feel insecure. This is not what you want to do in the beginning. Instead, *framing should be clear and non-threatening,* a way to introduce your peers to the goal of the experience.

More on identifying your goal and preparing your framing statement

So far, we've gone over how to identify your goal and how to begin the lesson with a prepared framing statement. Let's review these points with an example of another type of lesson that you as a peer leader might be presenting.

You have been asked to present a lesson to **twenty tenth**

graders on the issue of **working out differences with other students.**

Below is a format to follow as you prepare your lesson:

Topic/Issue: Conflict Resolution – Working out differences with others

Population & Number: Twenty sophomore students

Goal: Students will identify sources of conflict and possible solutions.

Framing Statement: *"Today we will identify common conflict situations which occur within our school. We will then explore ways of working out some of these differences. Our hope is that by understanding each other a little bit better, we can help make our school a better place."*

Read over our framing statement and check out if it:

- *Is specific or general*
- *Tells what the task or goal is*

What you say at the beginning of a lesson should help the students focus and relax so that they think "This won't be so bad." Then the chances of the students listening to what you have to say, and working with you successfully, are far greater.

Okay, so the lesson has been framed effectively. *Now what?*

Now it is time to figure out *how to reach your goal.*

3) Reaching Your Goal: *How will you accomplish your goal with the group?*

This is the "meat" of the lesson. Think of your goal as a *destination*.

- **How will you get there?**
- **What "route" will you take?**

Plan your lesson so that the students receive information and are actively involved.

Always combine **a little lecture** with **a lot of activity.**

So...Start by framing the lesson (explain the purpose of the session).

Then...Actively involve the students in a meaningful way.

Can you think of your favorite teachers? What is it exactly which makes them your favorite? Chances are that they do one of the following:

1) Involve you by having you express your thoughts to the class or other students.

2) Listen to what you have to say and treat you with respect.

3) The lessons or topics presented by them have meaning in your life.

Whenever you work with others, model your teaching after what works best for you. In other words: *actively involve the students in a meaningful way.*

Some of the ways to do this are:

- **small group discussion**
- **large group discussion**
- **brainstorming**
- **physical team builders**
- **ice-breakers**

We will offer specific ways of using each approach later in this guide.

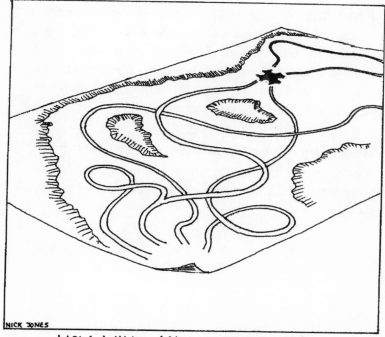

HOW WILL YOU GET THERE?

L et's see how we can involve students in the lesson we have already started to put together on Conflict Resolution.

So far we have studied:

Topic/Issue: Conflict Resolution – Working out differences with others.

Population & Number: Twenty sophomore students.

Goal: Students will identify sources of conflict and possible solutions.

Framing Statement: *"Today we will identify common conflict situations which occur within our school. We will then explore ways of working out some of these differences. Our hope is that by understanding each other a little bit better, we can help make our school a better place."*

Reaching Your Goal: Divide the class into groups of six. Have each group brainstorm a list of common situations which cause conflict between students.

After ten minutes, have one person from each group read their group's list aloud to the rest of the class.

After each list has been read, have the groups circle the commonalities on their sheets of paper.

Each group brainstorms a list of possible strategies to the common conflicts identified.

After ten minutes, have one person from each group read their group's list aloud to the rest of the class.

A natural way to end this lesson would be to have students individually write down one solution from the ones offered which they will try out the next time they find themselves in a conflict situation. In small groups the students could then share what strategy they have chosen.

The ending to a lesson is called *closure* and is probably the most important part of the lesson because it is the last thing people will remember.

Let's explore the idea of *closure* more completely.

4) Coming To Closure

Closure means a sense of completion.

Have you ever been on the telephone with someone and they hung up on you?

How did that make you feel?

This is an example of *not* having closure.

Students must never feel incomplete at the end of a learning session. If they do (maybe they are upset or worried), these feelings will preoccupy them for the rest of their day. A closure activity will not only help the students, but also clue the peer leader as to who needs some extra support.

Here is one way which we find to be extremely efficient in coming to closure:

- **At the close of a lesson make sure everyone can see each other and is listening.**
- **Have each student complete a sentence stem.**

A sentence stem is a statement left incomplete:

- *One thing I learned is...*
- *One thing that surprised me is...*
- *Right now I feel...*

To complete the sentence stems, each student has a turn, either in a circle (our preference) or by rows. It is best to give students three different sentence stems from which they may choose one. If someone needs a little more time, allow him/her to pass and take his turn later.

Here are some sentence stem completions you might hear at the close of the lesson on conflict resolution:

- *"One thing I learned is that sometimes saying you're sorry really helps."*
- *"One thing that surprised me is that others feel the same way I do."*
- *"Right now I feel happy because I found a friend that I thought I had lost."*

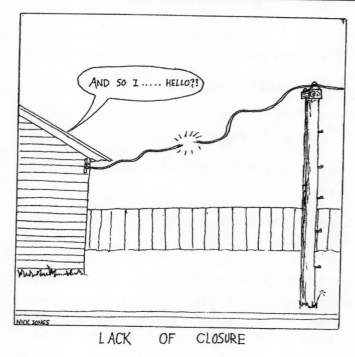

LACK OF CLOSURE

Some More Thoughts On Closure

Whenever you are working with a group of students, there is always a chance that someone will become upset during a lesson or immediately afterwards. If a student appears to be upset by his appearance, actions or words, you should discuss his feelings with him. If necessary, you should take him to a trained adult staff member who you, yourself, trust. Your role as a peer leader is to be a communicator, supporter, and friend, not to counsel someone through a problem in his or her life. The best thing you can do for someone with serious problems is to guide them to get the appropriate help (and that means someone who is professionally trained for just that purpose).

We have now covered the four components to help you put your thoughts into a complete lesson.

Here is the entire sample lesson plan:

Topic/Issue: Conflict Resolution – Working out differences with others.

Population & Number: Twenty sophomore students.

Goal: Students will identify sources of conflict and possible solutions.

Framing Statement: *"Today we will identify common conflict situations which occur within our school. We will then explore ways of working out some of these differences. Our hope is that by understanding each other a little bit better, we can help make our school a better place*

Reaching Your Goal: Divide the class into groups of six. Have each group brainstorm a list of common situations which cause conflict between students.

After ten minutes have one person from each group read their group's list aloud.

After each list has been read have each group individually circle the commonalities on their sheet of paper.

Groups then brainstorm a list of possible strategies to the common conflicts identified.

After ten minutes have one person from each group read their group's list aloud.

Closure: Have each student write down one specific strategy which he or she will use the next time a conflict situation arises. In the small groups, each student shares his or her strategy with the others.

After each individual has finished sharing, bring the entire group together and ask students to complete the sentence stem – " One thing I learned about conflict is..."

And there you have it. If you prepare for each presentation or lesson using this model, your chances of success will increase dramatically.

The following practice sheets provide the lesson format we have just introduced to you in simple form. Try completing the practice sheets on the next three pages. We have given you the beginning of a lesson that a peer leader would typically be asked to present. There are lesson plan blanks in the final section of this guide (page 110) for you to duplicate.

Practice sheet # 1

Topic/Issue: *Bicycle safety: The importance of wearing your helmet at all times.*

Population & Number: *25 fifth graders*

Goal:

_____

_____

_____

_____

Framing Statement:

_____

_____

_____

_____

_____

_____

_____

_____

Reaching Your Goal:

_____

_____

_____

_____

_____

_____

_____

_____

_____

Closure:

_____

_____

_____

_____

_____

_____

_____

_____

_____

_____

_____

Practice sheet # 2

Topic/Issue: *Adjustment to a new school: New students who do not know anyone.*

Population & Number: *15 incoming freshmen who moved into the area over the summer.*

Goal:

_____

_____

_____

_____

Framing Statement:

_____

_____

_____

_____

_____

Reaching Your Goal:

_____

_____

_____

_____

_____
_____
_____
_____
_____
_____
_____
_____
_____
_____
_____
_____
_____

Closure:

_____
_____
_____
_____
_____
_____
_____
_____
_____
_____
_____
_____
_____
_____

WORKING WITH GROUPS:
SOME CONSIDERATIONS

So, you have a plan and everything should run smoothly, right? Well, not exactly.

Groups are unique and unpredictable. You never can tell how people will respond to something new.

The challenge lies in helping the students to make connections between the lesson and their everyday experiences.

You want them to say aloud to the group or whisper things to their neighbor such as:

"Yeah, that happened yesterday."
"I was just saying that this morning."
"That happened to you didn't it?"

Connections will occur if the students are:

- Moving around and not sitting for too long

- Talking to each other as part of the experience

- Laughing and having fun as they learn

- Thinking about how the experience might effect their own lives.

The "trick," and we do mean trick, is to "grab" the students' attention from the start by doing something which creates a "feeling and response" from the group. This is not easy, but if you can do it amazing things can happen. We will show you some ways of creating what we call the "magic of connection" for your peers.

ABRACADABRA: The magic of connection

Have you ever had someone show you a magic trick? You know, like taking a rabbit out of a hat or figuring out the card you've chosen from the deck.

Successful tricks create a feeling and response from the audience. Something like...

"How'd you do that?" "Will you show me?"

If your peers are asking you questions like these during a lesson, you have succeeded in involving them and creating excitement.

You are listening for responses like...

"Oh wow"
"I see"
"I get it"
"Can we do that again?"

When students respond with statements like these in an excited tone it means that they are involved with the experience and are open to new ideas and discoveries.

Have you ever had someone show you how to do a magic trick?

Once you learned it, what did you do?

You probably did the same trick for as many people as you could find.

What if the students you were working with (your peers) wanted to show what they learned to as many people as possible?

That's what peer leadership is all about: **modeling for, and maximizing the involvement, of others.**

"Through my peer leadership workshops with younger children I know I at least helped one child by being an example."

Brenda Nimoh, age 16 and a member of Shea High School's "Student Bridges" Peer leaderhip Program in Pawtucket, Rhode Island.

"I feel younger kids should be involved in working with older kids. It's leading by example."

Frank Vaccaro, age 17 is a member of Rutland High School's "Peer To Peer" program, Rutland, Vermont.

HAVE YOU EVER HAD SOMEONE SHOW YOU A MAGIC TRICK?

IN THE COMFORT OF YOUR OWN
~~~~ ZONE ~~~~

Most people have a place where they feel safe and secure.

This place is called the Comfort Zone.

If people feel unsure or nervous when experiencing something new it is because they are being taken out of their comfort zone. A peer leader helps students stretch out of their comfort zone by modeling support and understanding. Stretching out of one's comfort zone is also called risk taking.

Visualize the last time you were in a social situation where you didn't know many people.

What was the first thing you did?
Did you look for someone you knew?
Someone who was familiar?
Someone who helped you get back into your "comfort zone"?

Maybe you took a risk and talked to someone you didn't know.

Some of the nicest people are those you haven't met yet.

Talking to a new person is an example of stretching out of your comfort zone.

Some of the most rewarding self-discoveries come when people do things they never imagined they could, or would do. One example might be doing a high ropes course for the first time. Have you ever been involved in an activity of this type? Compare how you felt before with how you felt after accomplishing the task. If you had a successful attempt after first being scared, you probably learned a lot about yourself.

At some time in the past you stretched out of your comfort zone. Whenever you stretch out of your comfort zone, growth is taking place.

An effective peer leader will help students stretch in a safe and supportive way.

When my father was teaching me how to swim, he would stand six feet away from me in the pool. As I would swim towards him, he would slowly take a few steps back. When I finally reached my destination, (his safe and secure arms), I found that I had gone ten feet without even realizing it until I had finished.

40

A peer leader does the same thing with new and potentially scary concepts and behaviors, offering just enough support while helping the students to discover that they could do more than they ever would have realized.

> *"Peer leadership was a humongous part of my high school participation . It changed my life completely. I used to be really shy. I wouldn't go up and introduce myself or express my feelings to anyone. Now I can open up myself, and that is important for me as I go along with my life into the future."*

Luke Barron, age 18, is a student at Roger Williams College in Rhode Island.

ESTABLISHING RAPPORT

Stretching students out of their comfort zone is not easy and it is one of the many challenges you face as a peer leader.

The first step is to *establish rapport*

Rapport is the feeling of connection people have with one another.

During a learning experience with your peers, establishing rapport means establishing a trusting give and take, working together and developing a sense of mutual respect.

This is accomplished by being honest and open with your peers. As a peer leader it is important to be respectful and non-judgemental and, most importantly, to listen to the people with whom you are working. We explore giving feedback on page 46.

"I have learned that your actions really do effect a lot of people and that a kind word can make a difference."

Prudence Daley, age 15, Pawling High School, Pawling, New York.

"This experience will stick with me forever, it was the best group I ever joined."

Melissa Basler, age 17, Pawling High School, Pawling, N.Y.

All people have one major need:

The need to belong

People need to feel that they are important to the functioning of the group. If each person believes that he/she is an integral part of what is happening, either through an idea they offer or a role they play in an activity, then the experience will have a greater chance for success.

People are fragile and always need to feel connected to the group. The peer leader is responsible for **modeling support and understanding.**

THE NEED TO BELONG

A LETTER FROM A STUDENT

"As a freshman and sophomore in high school I felt that everyone else was better than me. I was always a follower rather than a leader. I looked up to others and felt that I could not do things for myself. I felt this way about myself because I have nerve deafness in both ears. It was not until I became involved with the peer leadership groups that I began to have a new outlook on myself. I came to realize that despite my hearing loss, I could in fact make a difference for others and do things for myself. Helping those in need has been a truly rewarding experience, it can be a learning experience for everyone involved. Now that I have been in various leadership positions, I think people realize that I am just as normal as everyone else."

Krista Barbagallo

Age 19, is a former member of Rutland High School's "Peer Leadership Program", Rutland, Vermont.

Krista is currently a college student majoring in psychology *"in order to continue helping people and making a difference."*

VALIDATION

When people support and encourage you they are doing something called *validation*.

In a group or learning situation it is the peer leaders's job to **validate** all students in the group.

Validate means to help each person feel their individual self-worth as part of the group experience.

Validation comes directly from the types of statements a peer leader makes.

Here are some **validation** statements:

- *"Thanks for your answer!"*

- *"Yes!"*

- *"I like your idea."*

- *"That was a wonderful thing you did!"*

- *"Thanks for sharing your feelings!"*

- *"I admire your honesty."*

When offering a validation statement to an individual or to the group you are also doing something called "giving feedback."

GIVING FEEDBACK

Feedback is when you tell another person how his or her behavior is affecting the other people in the group.

Feedback is not a criticism, judgement or labeling. Instead, it is based on what you see or what you hear.

Check out the following example to see the difference between an **observation** and a **label.**

If during a learning session a student has not spoken for the first two hours and is alone during breaks, a skilled peer leader will notice.

Here is a **labeling** statement:

"That student is so shy."

Here is an **observation** of the same person

"That student has not spoken very often. I wonder if he knows anyone here? I'll go see if he's okay."

After noticing someone's behavior, it is how you **respond** which is important. Your **response** can help the group **move forward** and **support** individuals within the group.

This is the purpose of feedback!

Here are some more examples:

During a workshop four students who are good friends laugh during discussions, have side conversations, and appear not to be paying attention.

Here is a labeling and judgmental statement:

> *"Those students are so rude and uncoopera-tive. I wish they weren't here ruining this experience for everyone."*

Here is a different approach to the same group of students.

> *"Those students are only sitting with their friends. They are talking to each other during discussions and are not looking at the person presenting. I would like to try and involve them more. I think they would really enjoy this experience. I'll see what I can do."*

And now some feedback for the entire group:

If during a workshop the group keeps coming in late from breaks, here's an approach which probably wouldn't work too well:

> *"C'mon you guys, you gotta get here on time, okay?"*

Here's a feedback statement which might work a little better:

"I appreciate how hard you've all been working and I know it is a beautiful day out there. My concern is that we have to keep waiting to start because many of you are coming in late from breaks. We have so much to cover in a short time that I need your help so that we can accomplish everything. Please come in on time whenever we have a break."

Try writing a feedback statement to the following situation:

During an AIDS discussion with 30 seventh grade students, three students laugh each time someone asks a question.

The challenge is not to judge and overreact. You are there for the students and, if they are acting in a disruptive way, it is critical to understand the reason for their behavior. If you react with a labeling statement you could lose any chance of having rapport with the group.

THE "YOU" STATEMENT

A "you" statement is when a person tries giving feedback but gets into judging and labeling without realizing it.

Here's an example:

"You better stop being disrespectful."

The term "disrespectful" is a judgement. It is not a description of the behavior.

THE "I" STATEMENT

An "I" statement is a unique form of feedback. It is making a feedback statement for yourself and not for others.

Here's an example:

> *"I feel frustrated when you speak to the person next to you whenever I am speaking."*

The previous statement does not label or judge; instead, it tells how you feel and describes the behavior which is affecting you.

Here is another example:

> *"I feel awkward when people laugh at others."*

THE "YOU" STATEMENT

Check out the difference between an "I" statement and a "you" statement using the same situation: A student keeps challenging what you are doing during the learning experience.

• "You're so negative, you're always complaining."

• "I am glad you are sharing your concerns with me because it lets me know how I'm doing. I want this to be a valuable experience for you. I feel uncomfortable. Let's talk about how we can work together on this."

The difference between a label and an observation can be slight. Following are different feedback statements. Decide whether each one is a label or an observation by circling the response you think is correct. (Answers at bottom of page.)

"I feel upset when you talk to the person next to you during group discussions."

    label or observation

"Every morning when you ignore me you're being so rude."

    label or observation

"You're all so disagreeable!"

    label or observation

"Six students in this class arrived after we started this lesson."

    label or observation

As you've discovered, sometimes it can be tricky to decide whether you are labeling or merely saying what you see and what you hear. If you are coming from a caring place and don't overreact to situations and people, you will be fine.

(Answers: observation, label, label, observation.)

"There is a fine line between leadership and a power trip and a program like this helps split up the two."

Michael Coppinger is a member of Rutland High School's "Peer To Peer" program, Rutland, Vermont.

FACILITATING THE GROUP

The leader of the group acts as facilitator.

The Facilitator is someone who makes it easier for others to feel safe, be involved and learn.

Here are some things to consider when acting as a facilitator:

- Start each session off by explaining to the group why they've been brought together. What is the purpose?

- Inform students as to what is expected of them so that there will be no surprises.

- Be aware of the needs of the people in the group. Watch carefully for the way people are responding to various experiences.

- Be open with your own feelings.

- Allow yourself to be vulnerable (this helps build rapport).

- Never put yourself above or below the students.

- Never say "I am an expert." Remember that everyone is an integral part of the group experience and that each one of them is at a different place in his or her life.

- Show that you are human. It is okay to make a mistake.

- Demonstrate in actions and words. (This is called modeling.)

Even if you do all of these things, you will have little if any chance for success with the group if you do not practice one key skill:

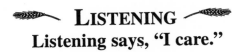

LISTENING
Listening says, "I care."

The most important and respectful communication skill a person can practice and develop is listening. If you think about those people in your life who you really love to hang out with (your closest friends), you will probably realize that they are the ones who listen to you when that is what you need from them.

Consider the following questions:

- What exactly do your friends do for you?
- How do you know they are truly listening to you?
- How do you know when people aren't listening to you?
- How does this make you feel?

Listening gives the following messages:

- *"I care."*
- *"Your ideas are important."*
- *"I am here for you."*

Imagine for a moment that you are in elementary or middle school and you are working with a high school student.

How would you feel if that high school student expressed the following messages to you?

- **I care**
- **Your ideas are important**
- **I am here for you**

You probably *would* feel important.

EFFECTIVE LISTENING

SOME GUIDELINES FOR EFFECTIVE
LISTENING

- Tune out the rest of the world. (Focus on the person speaking.)

- Use your eyes. (Watch the person speaking and maintain eye contact.)

- Be aware of your body posture. (Face the person, do not lean away or sit sideways.)

- Respond, do not react. (Take in the entire thought before saying anything.)

- Ask open-ended questions. (Questions which invite the person to share more information.)

- Check out with the person what they have said. (Tell them what you think you heard and ask them if that is accurate.)

PROCESSING WITH THE GROUP

When a group of people is experiencing something together, a process is taking place. In order to help each person (including yourself) understand what is happening, it is important to process with the group.

Processing means to examine what people are thinking and feeling.

Processing also helps to identify the reasons for doing certain activities and to help in understanding what people can learn from the activity.

Ways to process:
During the group experience, you can ask any of the following questions:

- *How are you feeling?*
- *What are you thinking?*
- *What did you learn?*
- *What is one word which describes the group?*
- *What is one thing that surprised you?*
- *What one thing do we need to change in order to be successful?*

Processing helps everyone to understand how the group is feeling and validates concerns some people may be having (especially if others in the group express similar concerns.) It is also a way of letting the group know that the session is one in which the trainer wants to know how people are feeling as well as what they are learning.

Speaking of processing, it's time to summarize some of the key ideas we have presented you in section I of this book, **"Working With Your Peers."**

➤➤ KEY IDEAS ◄◄

- **Peers:** Those in your same age group as well as younger students with whom you might be working.

- **Leadership:** Maximizing the involvement of others.

- **Peer leader:** A student who is involved in working with other students by making presentations, teaching lessons or being involved in helpful activities.

- **Framing an experience:** Giving a clear and specific introduction to the group at the beginning of a presentation or lesson. The purpose is to help everyone feel as relaxed as possible so that they can focus on the skills presented rather than on their fear of the unknown.

- **Reaching your goal:** The goal is like a destination for the group. The peer leader decides what route to take in order to arrive at the destination successfully.

- **Closure:** A sense of completion. It is critical for people to identify how they feel at the end of a learning experience. Closure activities are for this purpose.

- **Comfort zone:** The place where people feel safe and secure. The peer leader helps students "stretch" out of their comfort zone (risk taking) in order to learn new things about themselves.

- **Establishing rapport:** The peer leader has the challenge of establishing rapport with the group she or he is working with. Rapport means a positive relationship of trust and understanding.

- **Validation:** To support, encourage and appreciate individuals or the entire group. Often people will not feel complete until they are validated.

- **Feedback:** Telling another person how his or her behavior is effecting you or the other people in the group.

- **You statement:** A statement which starts with "you" usually turns into a judgement, label or criticism.

- **I statement:** A form of feedback which expresses how "I" feel or what "I" need. It is an effective way to avoid judging or labeling others in the group.

- **Facilitator:** Presents or teaches a lesson to the group. Makes the participants feel safe, involved and valued.

- **Processing:** Helps the group examine together what was experienced and why. It helps people understand what they learned, how they felt during the experience and why they felt certain ways. It is the most critical part of a lesson because it helps people understand how they and others are feeling, and is often the last thing people remember.

PRINCIPLES OF PEER
⚛ LEADERSHIP ⚛

A principle is the way a person believes people should act towards one another. People may identify the principles they choose to follow.

Here are some of our principles of peer leadership:

- Students can have tremendous impact on the lives of their peers.
- Students must be respectful of their peers.
- Students deserve to be listened to.
- Students should not be judged or labeled.
- Students should seek to understand differences between people.
- Students learn best when being guided towards what to do rather than being told what they should do.

A peer leader must live by specific principles. Let's explore why you consider certain people to be leaders.

Write down the names of three people who you consider to be leaders:

1. _____

2. _____

3. _____

What makes these people leaders? Write down some of the principles you feel have guided or guide their lives when they are/were working with others:

_____

_____

_____

_____

_____

_____

Write down your principles of peer leadership:

_____

_____

_____

Now share what you've written with another person and write
your principles on index cards (one principle per card).

Whenever you are about to make a presentation to a group,
review what you have written as a way to "focus" and remind
you of how you want to act towards others.

We like the way communications specialist **Carl Rogers**
talked about leadership and working with others in his book
"A Way of Being":

> *"A leader is best*
> *When people barely know that he exists,*
> *Not so good when people obey and*
> *acclaim him,*
> *Worst when they despise him...*
> *But of a good leader, who talks little,*
> *When his work is done, his aim ful-*
> *filled, They will all say, "We did this our-*
> *selves."*

═══ OUR HOPE ═══

It is our hope that as you apply the teachings from this book, you will inspire the students with whom you work to go out and do for others what you did for them; be supportive and understanding during new, scary, and sometimes difficult times.

The process of growth, accomplishment, and achievement is a never ending one, and is filled with many challenges. It is during these challenging times when a person needs support and encouragement the most. The awareness of when and how to offer support to others comes directly from the experiences of working with your peers in workshop or classroom situations. The skills gained from working with your peers are skills which will last a lifetime.

As we take you through the rest of *The Peer Partners Handbook,* we will offer specific activities to use with others as you continue to be part of the process of making a better world.

"The more students get involved, the less stereotyping there would be, and the more students would realize not to judge a person by their clothes, looks, or race. It is so important for students to notice that no one is better or worse than themselves. I learned all this through my school's peer leadership program."

Mokana Cooper, age 16, Shea High School, Pawtucket, Rhode Island.

II

Activities To Meet Your Needs

"I learned to teach people in fun ways that we all can get along."

Richard Pouliot, age 16, Shea High School, Pawtucket, Rhode Island

ACTIVITES TO
MEET YOUR NEEDS

We talked earlier about "reaching your destination" with the group. There are many choices open to you and it is the goal you have identified which helps you decide what activities to use with your peers.

In this section we will talk about the types of activities to consider. We will also give you some specific activities and offer a list of resources to use whenever you are planning a group experience with your peers. First, however, we'll talk a little about team building.

Before considering what to do with groups, it is important to understand why you are running activities at all. It revolves around the concept of team building. The next four pages will talk about team building as it relates to working with your peers.

ACTIVITIES TO MEET YOUR NEEDS

≋ TEAM BUILDING ≋

If a group is to be successful, it is critical for the students to be **respectful** and **understanding** of each other.

As a peer leader it is your role to provide the opportunity and know-how to bring the group together.

This is called team building.

There are two forms of team building:

- Small group team building

- Large group team building

"Every reliable relationship gives you the strength to carry on."

Dayna Barth, age 17, Rutland High School, Rutland, Vermont.

Small group team building helps to build human relations skills in a focused and intimate setting. It also allows for team members to speak and be listened to.

A time for small group team building would be when a group or team has to plan a specific activity or program, like a seventh grade orientation program.

Large group team building occurs during times when it is important for the entire group to have a shared experience.

An appropriate time for this would be when unity towards a cause is necessary, as in a club, leadership group, class, student council, etc.

Before embarking on a team building experience, ask yourself:

"What do I wish to accomplish with this group?"

Your answer will help determine the form of the team building experience you wish to facilitate, small group or large group.

There are two types of team building experiences:

Physical team building

Inter-personal team building

- **Physical team building is activity oriented with a possible physical challenge.**

- **Inter-personal team building is more intimate and focuses on listening to each other and sharing.**

Whether running a large or small group, physical or interpersonal team building experience, remember to always keep three things in mind:

- *Frame the experience*
- *Validate everybody*
- *Have a closure process ready*

We will now offer you sample activities for the two forms of team building (small group and large group), and some "icebreakers" to get the group warmed up and to help people feel a little more comfortable about being in the group. We also have provided you with the source for each activity (if we know it).

When possible, facilitate activites you are familiar with, ones you have done yourself. When in doubt, go to what is most familiar to you. If you haven't had much experience with activites like these, whenever possible, rehearse with a group receptive to helping you out, perhaps a planning group or peer leadership group of which you are a member.

NICK JONES!

SMALL GROUP TEAM BUILDING

LARGE GROUP TEAM BUILDING

Activity # 1: Silent Birthdays

Grades: 4–12

Number of students: Ten or more

Uses: Large group team building, ice-breaker

Time: Ten minutes

Purpose:
The purpose of this activity is to get people moving and communicating in a different way (without words). It is a non-threatening approach to begin group building (where people feel a part of what is happening).

Task:
The group's task is to have everyone line up in order of their birthday (date only not year born). The goal is to end up with a long line starting with January and going month by month, ending with December. This must be done silently, without words, meaning no writing on paper, the ground or in the air. People may communicate using only their fingers and a nod or shake of the head.

What the leader says:
"I would like you to line yourselves up in order of your birthdays. You must do this silently, no talking or writing on paper. Use only non-verbal signals like motioning or signaling with hands or fingers. Have January start here (pick a spot and point to it) and have December end here (again, pick a spot). After you've all lined up, we'll check to see how you did. If someone is having trouble finding their month, you may help them out as long as you do so non-verbally."

Processing:

After the line is formed, start at January and have each student call out his or her birthday. If someone is out of order or in the wrong month, model support and help find the appropriate space. After going through the entire line (or year) ask some of the following questions, or questions of your own:

1. *What was it like not being able to speak?*
2. *What was challenging about it?*
3. *How do you usually communicate with others?*
4. *What did you learn about communication?*
5. *Who found someone with the same birthday?*

Closure statement:

"As we work together, it's important to remember how challenging it can be sometimes to understand another person. Sometimes you think another person means one thing and she is actually saying something else. How many of you have ever had another person misunderstand what you were saying? Has anyone ever had someone finish your sentence for you? How did you feel? This shows how important effective communication is. Thank you. Let's move on to our next activity."

Final thoughts:

People are not used to communicating without talking. Even though you tell them not to speak, some will anyway. A gentle reminder is important but not in a "scolding" tone. If you have to remind people to communicate without words, talk about it with the group afterwords while processing.

Source: We don't know where this one came from. We've been doing "Silent Birthdays" for a long time, but similar activites can be found in the book * "Playfair" by Matt Weinstein and Joel Goodman.

* *See "Additional Resources" on page 105 for a description for this and all other sources we mention.*

Activity # 2: Incorporations

Grades: 4-12

Number of students: Twenty or more

Uses: Ice-breaker

Time: Ten minutes

Purpose:
The purpose of this activity is to increase the general energy level of the group by getting people to move around, mix and have fun.

Task:
The group's task is to form and reform groups as quickly as possible based on directions from the leader. For example, the leader might say, *"Form a group with everyone who uses the same brand of toothpaste as you do."* People will start shouting out their toothpaste brand until they find others who use the same kind. Another direction the leader might give is, *"Find all the other people here who were born in the same season as you"* and people would start shouting out their season.

INCORPORATIONS

What the leader says:

"We're going to play a game called "Incorporations." It's a really easy game about forming and reforming groups as quickly as possible. I'll shout out a group for you to get into. Then as quickly as possible, get into the group I've given you. When you hear the signal (have something like a slide whistle or noise maker, the funnier the better) stop, and I'll give you the next group. Ready?"

- *Get into groups of 3*

- *Groups of 3 plus 1*

- *Groups of 5 and each person in the group must have one item of clothing which is the same color*

- *Think of the last digit of your phone #, find everyone with the same last digit in their phone #*

- *Groups of 8 and form the letter H with your bodies*

- *Find everyone who was born in the same month you were born in.*

Processing: After groups have formed, start with January and call out each month in order right up to December. Each group should cry out when you say their birthday month name. If there are two groups for the same month, help them find each other so that in the end there are only twelve groups.

Have each month (group) separately form a circle in order of the group members' birthdays (month and day, not year). If someone has a birthday on the day you are giving the workshop, have the group acknowledge it by wishing that person a happy birthday.

Closure statement:

"Okay, make sure you learn the names of the people on your right and on your left. Please introduce yourself to those people now. Thank the people in your month and let's move on to the next activity..."

Final thoughts:

People love this high-energy mixer. They get to meet others in the group, laugh and have fun. We like doing this one early on with a group because it is low-risk, high energy and starts connecting people. You can make up your own groups for people to get into based on who you're working with. Remember to get something to signal with. (Slide whistles can be found at most music stores.)

Source: "Playfair" by: Matt Weinstein & Joel Goodman.

Activity # 3: Human Treasure Hunt

Grades: 4–12

Number of students: 10 or more

Uses: Large group team builder, ice-breaker

Time: Forty minutes

Purpose:
The purpose of this activity is for people to mix with one another, learn about each other, make connections, be actively involved and to practice their listening skills.

Task:
Students are to use human treasure hunt sheets (see next page) to find people in the group who fit the specific criteria listed on the sheets. Criteria might include someone who is from another state, or someone who has more than one younger sibling. Once someone fits a certain criteria, (and the only way to find out is to ask), have that person sign the sheet.

What the leader says:
"Today we're going on something called a human treasure hunt. The treasures you'll be looking for can be found right in this group. The purpose of this activity is to meet others in this group and learn something about them. We will give you a human treasure hunt sheet and a pencil. Then get started. Try to connect with as many people as possible. Keep going until we stop you."

Human Treasure Hunt

1. Find 3 people who have more than 12 letters in their first and last names combined.

2. Find someone whose favorite season is winter.

3. Find someone who paints.

4. Find 4 people who read *Calvin and Hobbes* every day.

5. Find 2 people who are vegetarians.

6. Find 2 people who have lived in another country.

7. Find someone who watches television less than 2 hours per week.

8. Find 3 people who rollerblade.

9. Find someone who likes working with others. Spend some time talking with that person as he/she tells you about it.

10. Find someone who you've never spoken to before. Have that person tell you something she/he does well.

11. Find someone who has the same size thumb as you do.

12. Find someone you haven't spoken with yet and together invent an unusual handshake.

   * Thanks to Joel Goodman and Matt Weinstein for the format of these questions.

Processing:

After 25 minutes have the group form a circle and ask each student to tell the group something they learned about another member in the group. After all have had an opportunity to speak, ask the students some or all of the following questions:

1. *What skills did you use during this exercise?*

2. *What surprised you?*

3. *In school you see some people all year long and never speak to them, why?*

Closure statement:

"Thanks for doing this activity with us. We hope that you can see that you don't always know what people are like unless you talk to them, show interest and listen."

Final thoughts:

This activity is fun. It is a good way for people to learn information about each other, which is useful if a group is going to be working together. We have provided you with one human treasure hunt sheet, but feel free to create your own set of questions – one which might better meet the needs of your group.

Source: "Playfair" Matt Weinstein, Joel Goodman

BRAINSTORMING
⇒⇒⇒ FOR ALL OCCASIONS ⇐⇐⇐

Skills: Sharing of ideas with others, working creatively together, respecting other people's ideas.

Uses: Generate ideas quickly from a large group efficiently. Get a sense of what people have learned or how they feel after a learning experience or after creative problem solving activity.

Framing Statement:
"Many of you have probably done brainstorming before. It literally means a storm of ideas. I'll ask a question and you respond. I'll write your answers on the paper. The goal is to get as many ideas as possible. There are no wrong ideas, every thought you have is correct because it is what you are thinking or feeling."

Procedure:
Put a piece of chart paper on a wall or use an easel or chalkboard. Ask the group a question and write down people's ideas on the paper or board with no discussion. After all the ideas are written, go back over the list and have students clarify their ideas if necessary so that everyone understands what each person was thinking.

Closure:
Thank everyone for their ideas and tell everyone that if they didn't share their ideas that's okay too. Depending on the purpose of the brainstorming, either keep the list posted, or move on to the next step to use the ideas generated.

THANK YOU

Never underestimate the power of these words.

When someone shares an answer in front of a group, large or small, they are risking not belonging.

So... always show sincere appreciation like....

"Thanks for going first"
or:
"Thank you" (plain and simple)

Remember:

THE LITTLE THINGS ARE
THE BIG THINGS

Once safety in the group is felt, more people will open up and the team building begins.

Activity #4: On/ Off Buttons

Grades: 8–12

Number of students: 6–12

Uses: Small group team building

Time: Thirty minutes

Purpose:
The purpose of this activity is to increase each group member's awareness of the needs of other group members and to establish guidelines to use when working together.

Task:
Through brainstorming, students in the group identify their likes (on buttons) and dislikes (off buttons) when working in a group.

What the leader says:
"Before we begin working on our project (or whatever it is the group is working on), it is important that we do some team building so that we can accomplish things in a way which makes people feel good about being a part of this group. We're going to do a brainstorm to learn more about the other people in this group. Please answer the following question and I'll write down what people say:"

"What turns you off about working in a group?"
"Please remember there is no one right answer. All answers or ideas are correct because they reflect how each of you feels." (Let this go for about 10-15 responses.)

"Okay, let's move onto a more positive question:"
"What turns you on about working in a group, in other words: what do you enjoy most about being in a group?"
(Let this go for about 10-15 responses and then continue.)

Processing:
After brainstorming both lists, ask students to explain their answers more clearly if necessary. Use open ended questions when having students explain their answers. For example:

"What did you mean by "bossy people?"

Closure statement:
"What we have here is a list of the needs people have if they are going to work successfully in this group. It is important to remember what people need, especially if things aren't going well which does *happen sometimes. If you ever find your-selves doing a lot from the "off" list, that's the time to stop working on* **what** *you're doing and instead focus on* **how** *you are doing it. The time you spend on understanding each other is the most important part of working with others."*

Final thoughts:
It is important to get as many ideas and thoughts as possible. Remember to encourage all to give input to the questions. This activity can tell you a lot about what people need and how they see their role in a group. Save the lists and encourage the group to review them whenever they start working together. Add to the list when necessary.

This is a natural lead-in to the next activity, "Human knot," which we recommend you do in combination with "On/Off Buttons."

Activity #5: Human Knot

Grades: 4–12

Number of students: 6–12

Uses: Small group team building

Time: Twenty minutes

Purpose:
The purpose of this activity is to increase group members' awareness of themselves and others in the group, and to feel a stronger sense of connection to other team members.

Task:
Ask the group to face each other in a tight circle. Each person holds out his right hand and grasps the right hand of someone else as if they were shaking hands. Each person then extends his left hand and grasps the hand of someone else so that each person is holding hands with two different people. The result should be a confusing configuration of arms and bodies (a human knot). The group must untangle the web of arms into a hand-in-hand circle. People may not let go of hands as they work together as a group.

What the leader says:
"We're going to do something called 'human knot.' Form a circle and reach out your right hand like you are going to shake hands with somone else in the circle. Gently grasp a hand with a person in your group who is not standing next to you. Hold onto that hand and grasp the left hand of another person so you are holding hands with two different people. Now, without letting go, and being gentle with the people whose hands you are holding, your challenge as a team is to untangle yourselves into a hand holding circle. Ready? Begin..."

HUMAN KNOT

Processing:
This team challenge can be frustrating for some groups. The key in processing is to have people express what it was like to work together as a group.

Ask people some or all of the following questions:

- *What was this experience like?*

- *What skills were necessary as you worked on this task?*

- *How might this experience help your team as you work together in the future?*

- *What surprised you as you worked on untangling the human knot?*

- *What did you learn?*

End by having team members express their appreciation to each other in the form of handshakes, hugs and thank you's.

Closure statement:
"Thank you for working so hard on this activity. As you continue to work together as a team, you will be able to accomplish a great deal if you have understanding of one another and act with care and concern."

Final thoughts:

This activity should be done after the group has had time to work together in other team building activities. It is part of the process of team building and can be frustrating and tense. If a team is having difficulty and does not appear to be moving towards success, untie part of the knot by allowing two people to release one hand with each other. This makes the task slightly easier. Some groups want to keep going until they untangle the web of bodies. Remember to remind the students that there is a delicate hand on the other end of their grip. You do not want people getting hurt as part of the experience.

Source: Silver Bullets by Karl Rohnke

Activity #6 Hidden Talents

Grades: 8–12

Number of students: 5–12

Uses: Small group team building

Time: Fifty minutes

Purpose:

The purpose of this activity is to increase group members' awareness of themselves and others in the group, and to feel a stronger sense of connection to other team members.

Task:

Each person individually writes down one talent or skill which he/she brings to the group. Students should think of something which others might not know about them. It is helpful if the peer leader offers some personal examples such as: "I'm good at getting things done," or "I listen well to others."

After each student writes down a talent, the peer leader has people share using the following approach:

1) Have the students seat themselves in a circle with the peer leader a part of the circle.

2) Before each person shares, the others in the group "guess" aloud what they think that person wrote down as her/his talent. After all the guesses are given the student reads what he/she actually wrote. Each turn is taken in this way:

- **all guess a hidden talent for one person**

- **that person shares what is actually written**

- **move onto the next until all have had a turn.**

It is appropriate for the peer leader to have a turn if the group requests it.

What the leader says:

"Today we're going to do a team building activity called 'Hidden Talents.' The purpose of this activity is to get to know each other a little bit better and to practice your listening skills at the same time."

"Each team of people is made up of talented and different individuals who come together to work towards a goal. Each person is an important resource. It is important to understand each team member as much as possible in order to achieve success, (Refer to "On /Off buttons" here if you have done this with the group). *I would like each of you to take a piece of paper (or index card) and write down one thing you do which can help this group succeed, a talent of some kind. An example might be 'I'm good at getting things done,' or 'I'm a good listener.'"*

86

"I would like you to take some time to do this right now. If you can't think of one or you're blanking out, relax and one may come to you. Otherwise, you'll have a chance to hear from others in the group. Sometimes other people can help point out the things you do which they appreciate."

HIDDEN TALENTS

Processing:

As each person says what she/he wrote down as a talent or skill, inconspicuously write it down next to their name on a piece of paper. After all have shared and received feedback from others in the group, read back the list of skills which the group possesses and ask:

"If we are able to put all these skills together, will we able to accomplish the tasks presented to us?"

The response most likely will be a positive one and the team will feel more connected than before you started. Then go around to each person and ask for a feeling word. Most should be positive, but if someone offers a word different in tone from the others, use your facilitation skills and check that person out after the others have spoken. If you feel someone needs more support, make sure you or someone else gives it to them after the session is over.

Final thoughts:

This is a wonderful experience to facilitate because it offers people the unique opportunity to say positive things to each other and to hear positive thoughts as well. Some students may find it difficult or embarrassing to hear good things about themselves. If this is true, it offers you a rich topic to talk about: *"Why is it so difficult to hear positive feedback?"* This in itself could become another discussion for another occasion when you have enough time to come to closure.

Special thanks to Bob Barrette for this one.

Activity # 7: Wheel In A Wheel:

Grades: 6–12

Number of students: 14 or more

Uses: Large group team building, ice breaker

Time: Forty – Sixty minutes

Purpose:
The purpose of this activity is for students to practice their listening skills, meet new people and talk to their peers about important issues in their lives.

Task:
Students are to form two tight circles (with equal numbers in each), one inside circle and one outside circle. People on the inside circle face out, and people on the outside circle face in. Students stand face to face with one another to form individual pairs.

The next step is to ask questions to the people on the inside circle and have the people on the outside circle act as listeners. Their job is to listen and ask open-ended questions. Inside people answer and outside people listen. After two or three minutes, stop the group and reverse roles. The outside person now answers and the inside person listens.

After each person has answered the same question, students on the outside circle move two places to the right so they have a new partner. Start the process over again. You may want to alternate who starts first (meaning on the second question have the outside people answer first while the inside people act as listeners).

What the leader says:

"We are going to take you through an activity called "Wheel in a Wheel." It is an opportunity for you to practice your listening skills and to work with other people."

"Let's count off please by 1's and 2's. All number 1's please form a tight circle, shoulder to shoulder facing in. Now all of the number 2's come over and stand behind someone in the circle. People on the inside turn around and face the person behind you. Introduce yourself if you do not know each other."

"I will ask the people on the inside a question. Outside people, your job is to listen and ask open-ended questions to learn more. All you do is listen. Keep going until I stop you (do you have your slide whistle yet?), *and then we will reverse roles. Ready? Inside people here's your first question..."*

Wheel In A Wheel Questions

1. *Talk about a place you would like to visit.*
2. *What do you do well?*
3. *What awards have you received or would you like to receive?*
4. *What is something you feel good about?*
5. *One of my goals is...*
6. *What person's life have you influenced for the good?*
7. *How do you usually react when you are criticized?*
8. *Where do you feel totally accepted?*
9. *What do you look for in a friend?*
10. *Select a word that you feel describes people your own age?*
11. *What talent should you develop?*
12. *What first impression do you give to others?*
13. *What first impression did you give to your last partner?*

14. What prevents you from giving an accurate first impression to others?

* Choose the questions which you feel will work with the group. Use all of them or write your own.

Processing: Have students respond to the following sentence stems starting with one person and going around in order from right to left. Students may pass on their turn in order to think about their answers.

- I learned...

- I feel...

- I wonder...

If the group you are working with is larger than 14, break students up into equal groups not exceeding 8.

Closure statement:
"Thank you for your cooperation. This activity shows how powerful the skill of listening is. When someone is listening to you, the message that someone cares really comes through. Imagine what our school could be like if all people truly listened to one another."

Final Thoughts:
Students may feel uncomfortable at first while going through the "Wheel in a Wheel." Observe how people react and offer support when you feel it is needed. Eventually, the supportive climate will help students feel relaxed as the activity continues. This is a marvelous mixer and skill builder to use with any group and with larger numbers.

Source: *Peer Leadership* by Thomas Turney

Activity # 8: Either/Or

Grades: 6–8

Number of students: 5–12

Uses: Small group team building

Time: 40 minutes

Purpose:
The purpose of this activity is to increase students' awareness of themselves and others, and to practice their listening skills.

Task:
Each student receives an Either/Or sheet (see next page) to fill out. After they have filled out the sheets, students sit in a circle and each shares his/her responses with the group. Responses are shared from beginning to end. As the answers are shared, the rest of the students listen.

After all have had a turn, items which need clarification are discussed. Here are some of the types of clarifications you might hear: *"Dave, you said you're more like summer than winter. What do you like to do in the summer?"* or *"You said you're more like a mountain than a valley because you feel you can see a lot of things. Could you tell me more, I'm not sure I understand."*

What the leader says:
"Today we're going to do a communication activity in which we'll be listening to each other and learning about one another. To do this I would first like each of you to individually fill out these Either/Or sheets. Take your time and don't worry about whether your answer is right or not. I want you to write whatever you feel as you read through the sheets. After everyone's finished, you will all have an opportunity to share with the group."

Either/Or

"Answer each of the following questions. Circle one of the responses and write a because statement to explain your choice. To make a choice, think of one of the characteristics you have which is similar to the answer you chose."

1. *Are you more like the country or the city?*

2. *Are you more like the summer or the winter?*

3. *Are you more like breakfast or dinner?*

4. *Are you more like a pickup truck or a sports car?*

5. *Are you more like a babbling brook or a quiet lake?*

6. *Are you more like a mountain or a valley?*

7. *Are you more like a mystery novel or a do-it-yourself book?*

8. *Are you more like a "No fishing" or a "Public fishing" sign?*

Processing: After all students have shared their answers in a circle ask if anyone has any answers they would like clarified. After a brief discussion, ask the following questions:

- *Which comparison was your favorite and why?*
- *What was it like to share your answers with others?*
- *What was it like to hear what others had to say?*
- *What is one thing you learned?*
- *What is one thing that surprised you?*
- *After doing this activity, how do you feel?*

Closure statement:
"Thank you for doing this activity and for listening so carefully to each other. I hope we can do more activities like this one because it is a great opportunity to learn more not only about others but ourselves as well."

Final thoughts:
This team builder is most appropriate for younger students especially grades 6–8. It is more focused than "Hidden Talents" because students have a chance to write their answers first before sharing.

Source: We don't know where this one comes from. We learned it from our friend Bob Barrette. There are similar activities in the book "Meeting Yourself Halfway" by Dr. Sidney B. Simon.

Activity # 9: Kitchen Kapers

Grades: 4–12

Number of students: 8–12

Uses: Small group team building

Time: 30 minutes

Purpose:
The purpose of this activity is for students to have fun, work together, and practice their communication and problem solving skills while working on a team creation.

Task:
The group is given an envelope filled with the following materials:

- 2 index cards
- 4 toothpicks
- 2 paper clips
- 2 pencils
- 1 rubber band
- 1 balloon

Once the group has the materials, they are given 15 minutes to invent a kitchen item that "no kitchen should be without." The more "way out" the idea the better. (All items in the envelope must be used.)

After 15 minutes, the team is given 5 minutes to come up with a commercial to sell its product.

What the leader says:
"I am going to give a sealed envelope to your team. When I give you the signal, open the envelope and using all of the contents, your team is to invent a wild and crazy kitchen item that no kitchen should be without. You will have 15 minutes to do this. Remember to involve everyone and listen to all ideas. Okay, open the envelopes and invent away."

After 15 minutes continue:

"Okay, you now have 10 minutes to come up with a commercial to sell your item. Again involve all of the people on your team in some way..."

Processing:

After the group has presented its commercial, process by asking some or all of the following questions:

- *Did your invention change as you worked on it and if so, how?*

- *How did you come up with your final idea?*

- *Was everyone involved in some way?*

- *What roles did people play?*

- *Did you have a leader?*

- *Was a leader necessary? Why or why not?*

- *How did you feel when you completed your invention?*

- *How do you feel now?*

Closure statement:

"Thank you for working so well together. Sometimes when you have a time-limit to do something it becomes more difficult to work with others because there is more pressure to accomplish the task. It is important to remember to ask yourself, 'Is it more important to accomplish the task or be a strong and supportive team?' If you have a strong and supportive team (and it takes a lot of work) you can make it through anything. Would you thank your teammates? Thanks to all of you again."

Final thoughts: This is a high energy activity and a lot of fun. It is important to be aware of quiet students who could pull back from dominant team members. If you see this happening, bring it up later in the processing. The most important learning in this activity comes from the processing. Be sure to give yourself enough time for closure.

Source: *Tribes Curriculum* and Thomas Turney

KITCHEN KAPERS

III

Helpful Hints

"The program helped me to trust people and not think of myself first all of the time."

Chantil Brown, age 18, is a member of Shea High School's "Student Bridges" peer program, Pawtucket, Rhode Island.

GETTING YOUR MATERIALS
TOGETHER

As we have mentioned numerous times throughout this guide, there are many challenges to being a peer leader. When working with people, you may encounter issues brought in by others which are beyond your control. You do the best you can.

In preparing to facilitate a class, remember:

The little things are the big things.

The little things can make or break a learning experience. If you are ready things will flow more smoothly and you'll be able to focus your energy on people and not things.

As a peer leader responsible for the group, you don't want the setting getting in the way. Logistics must be considered.

99

LOGISITICS

Logistics means taking care of everything which you have control over, *before* the experience.

Be aware of the following:

- The number of people in the group.
- The flow of what you will cover (the activities you plan to use and in what order).
- The setting: Do you want the desks in straight rows? Do you want the students sitting in chairs in a circle? Do you want them sitting on the floor?
- Materials : What materials do you need?

Here are some standard materials which should always be available:

- chart paper (newsprint)
- magic markers (non-toxic)
- masking tape
- name tags (preferably not ones which say *"my name is"*)
- index cards
- pads of paper
- pencils *

* Remember when we said the little things are the big things? If in the beginning of the lesson someone in the group does not have a pencil and you have one for them, right away you are showing support and that person will not feel isolated.

LOGISTICS

PROCESSING WITH YOUR ADVISOR

Whenever you finish doing a presentation, or facilitating a class or workshop, it is important to get closure for yourself. It takes a lot of energy to work with others. All the listening and observing, speaking and processing begin to take their toll after a while. In other words, you can get pretty emotionally tired. That's the time to take care of yourself and each other. We advise you to always work with at least one other peer leader whenever possible.

After a session which you have facilitated, always process with your advisor. We like the following approach which we learned from our good friend Tom Turney.

Sit down as a group and answer the following questions:

- **What are two things you did well?**
- **What is one thing you could have done differently?**
- **What is something you needed from your advisor or teammates which would have helped you to be more affective?**

After each person has had a chance to answer and clarify what they said, spend some time talking about things, making sure everyone is feeling okay. Then talk about how you as a group could improve next time you work together (this is a team building process.)

Working Without a Program (Some Direction):

There is always a need to help others, whether it's younger students, senior citizens or in community service. If you are not part of an official group or club, and you don't have an advisor, look for an adult who can open the door for you. Let your actions take care of the rest. Pretty soon people will come to you offering their assistance.

PROCESSING WITH YOUR ADVISOR

IV

Additional Resources

The following section talks about some of our favorite resources, how to get them, and some of our favorite activities from each.

ADDITIONAL RESOURCES

Playfair, Everybody's Guide to Noncompetitive Play, by Matt Weinstein & Joel Goodman

This is our favorite book for noncompetitive games and activites to build community and connection between people. The games are tried and true and are winners every time. The instructions are easy to follow and it contains valuable information regarding cooperation and working together.

Available from:

Sagamore Institute
110 Spring Street
Saratoga Springs, NY 12866.

Playfair

amoeba tag	hum dinger
back to back dancing	imaginary ball toss
birthdays	1-2-3-4
finger dancing	roll playing
human spring	five changes

105

Peer Leadership, A Human Relations Process to Reduce Substance Abuse and Improve School Climate, by Thomas Turney

This is the best resource there is on peer leadership, peer programming and peer human relations activites. It is a resource which every peer program should have because it provides opportunities for skill building and practice, planning, and problem solving as well as how to design a peer leadership workshop.

Available from:
>Thomas Turney
>354 Central Avenue
>Mountainside, NJ   07092

Peer Leadership

alligator river	comfort and caring
community meeting	desert survival
gift of happiness	life line
murder mystery	people in my life
public interview	weekly reaction sheet
line revolution	developing the next meeting

Silver Bullets, A Guide To Initiative Problems, Adventure Games and Trust Activities, by Karl Rohnke

This book is filled with a variety of group challenges to meet your every need. The activities are clearly described with words, pictures and diagrams. We highly recommend this book if you run team building activities with groups.

Available from:

> Project Adventure, inc.
> PO box 100
> Hamilton, MA   01936

Silver Bullets

moonball

trust fall

group juggling

triangle tag

fire in the hole

braaaaaaaack-whfffff

hog call

everybody's it

toss-a-name-game

circle the circle

Meeting Yourself Halfway,
by Dr. Sidney B. Simon

This book contains 31 small group activities to help people in understanding themselves and others. It is an excellent resource when preparing to run a small group team building experience.

Available from:
> The Sagamore Institute
> 110 Spring Street
> Saratoga Springs, NY   12866

Meeting Yourself Halfway

am I somone who	do you
priorities	things I am proud of
slice of life	coat of arms
who are all those others	contracts with myself

V

Sample Lessons,
Blank Lesson Sheets

Preparing for the presentation

Topic/Issue: The way people treat others

Population & Number 30 10th & 11th grade students

Goal: To come up with solutions to put more people up instead of putting them down.

Framing
Statement: "Today we will talk about the way people treat others. Your ideas are important as we find ways to help each other out. We'll start by listening to a song which is a true story about a student who is made fun of."

Reaching Your
Goal: 1) Play song: "Howard Gray" - Reveal a story where you personally were put down (don't get too personal). Ask them if they have a story (take 2 or 3)
2) Put up 4 newsprint headers that say "How do people feel when they get put down?"
3) Explain brainstorm and divide up into four groups - have them brainstorm
4) Bring all lists to the front - read and compare.
5) Why do people get put down? (Whole group brainstorm)
6) If people are continually put down, what happens to them? (brainstorm extreams)
7) Show your list from peer leaders (write this on newsprint ahead of time) - lose self-esteem, believe what people say, suicidal, anorexia, become introverted, put others down, drugs/alcohol, run away

Closure: Ask students: "What can you do to put people up instead of down?"

Make a plan and vote on a solution for everyone in the group.

Lesson by:
Jayne Harrington

Preparing for the presentation

Topic/Issue: Junior high school transition into high school

Population & Number: Approx. 100-200 Jr. high students

Goal: Have Junior high students meet students from neighboring Jr. highs with whom they will be attending high school. We will do this at a Junior high dance.

Framing
Statement: "We have invited you to this dance to give you the opportunity to meet your future classmates."

Reaching Your
Goal: We will run "People Search" & "incorporations" at the beginning of the dance to encourage students to interact with students they are not familiar with rather than their "best friends."

Closure: "Before you leave tonight we would like to give you the opportunity to talk with your fellow classmates about high school and any anxieties you may have about the transition into high school."

Lesson by:
Amy Densmore &
Shannon Haley

111

PREPARING FOR THE PRESENTATION

Topic/Issue:

_____

_____

Population & Number

_____

_____

Goal:

_____

_____

_____

_____

Framing Statement:

_____

_____

_____

_____

_____

_____

_____

_____

_____

Reaching Your Goal:

_____

_____

_____

_____

_____

_____

_____

_____

_____

_____

_____

_____

Closure:

_____

_____

_____

_____

_____

_____

_____

_____

_____

_____

_____

_____

PREPARING FOR THE PRESENTATION

Topic/Issue:

_____

_____

Population & Number

_____

_____

Goal:

_____

_____

_____

_____

Framing Statement:

_____

_____

_____

_____

_____

_____

_____

_____

_____

_____

Reaching Your Goal:

_____

_____

_____

_____

_____

_____

_____

_____

_____

_____

_____

_____

_____

Closure:

_____

_____

_____

_____

_____

_____

_____

_____

_____

_____

_____

_____

ABOUT THE AUTHORS

Jerry **Kreitzer** is a teacher, inventor, and state legislator. He created the peer leadership program at Rutland High School, Rutland Vermont, in 1980 and continues to direct this program. He also teaches communications and works as district prevention coordinator. He has served in the Vermont State Legislature since 1991. He has received numerous awards including the *Sallie Mae Teacher Tribute Award* in 1989.

David **Levine** is a teacher, facilitator, musician, and songwriter. He co-authored *The Road Best Traveled* social skills program (1991), and *Through the Eyes of Howard Gray* (1992). He has worked with students conducting communication workshops from Maine to New York to the island of Guam. His recording *Dance of a Child's Dreams* on Angel Records, won the *Parent's Choice Gold Award* in 1993. David lives with his wife Devi near Woodstock, New York.

ABOUT THE ARTISTS

Nick Jones recently graduated from Amherst College in Massachusetts with a B.A. in philosophy. In addition to being a cartoonist, he is an active jazz musician and computer programmer. Jones lives in Randolph, Vermont.

Karen Seeland is founder and president of K•V•S GRAPHICS. She is the mother of three and resides in Beachwood, New Jersey.

Information on training workshops for students can be obtained from the authors at the following address:

Jerry Kreitzer & David Levine
69 Nichols Street
Rutland, Vermont 05701

NOTES

NOTES

NOTES

NOTES

NOTES

NOTES

NOTES

NOTES